SPORTS' GREATEST OF ALL TIME

SOCCER'S G.O.A.T.

PELE, LIONEL MESSI, AND MORE

JON M. FISHMAN

Lerner Publications ◆ Minneapolis

Copyright © 2020 by Lerner Publishing Group, Inc.

All rights reserved. International copyright secured. No part of this book may be reproduced, stored in a retrieval system, or transmitted in any form or by any means—electronic, mechanical, photocopying, recording, or otherwise—without the prior written permission of Lerner Publishing Group, Inc., except for the inclusion of brief quotations in an acknowledged review.

Lerner Publications Company
A division of Lerner Publishing Group, Inc.
241 First Avenue North
Minneapolis, MN 55401 USA

For reading levels and more information, look up this title at www.lernerbooks.com.

Main body text set in Aptifer Sans LT Pro.
Typeface provided by Linotype AG.

Library of Congress Cataloging-in-Publication Data

Names: Fishman, Jon M., author.
Title: Soccer's G.O.A.T. : Pele, Lionel Messi, and more / Jon M. Fishman.
Other titles: Soccer's GOAT | Soccer's greatest of all time
Description: Minneapolis : Lerner Publications, 2020. | Series: Sports' greatest of all time | Includes bibliographical references and index. | Audience: Age 7–11. | Audience: Grade 4 to 6.
Identifiers: LCCN 2018044380 (print) | LCCN 2018045987 (ebook) | ISBN 9781541556348 (eb pdf) | ISBN 9781541556003 (lb : alk. paper)
Subjects: LCSH: Soccer players—Biography—Juvenile literature. | Women soccer players—Biography—Juvenile literature.
Classification: LCC GV942.7.A1 (ebook) | LCC GV942.7.A1 F54 2020 (print) | DDC 796.334092/2 [B]—dc23

LC record available at https://lccn.loc.gov/2018044380

Manufactured in the United States of America
7-52959-43472-6/1/2023

CONTENTS

Denmark (*front left*) and the Netherlands have competed in the Women's World Cup since it began in 1991.

KICKOFF!

When you watch soccer, do you try to pick out the best players on each team? Do you ever ask your friends or family what they think? You probably don't always agree. That's part of the fun of sports. Everyone has opinions. There's a lot to think about when it comes to who is the greatest of all time (G.O.A.T.). Soccer has a long history, and people play the game all around the world.

FACTS AT A GLANCE

In 1990, **FRANZ BECKENBAUER** became only the second person to win the World Cup as both a player and a manager.

MIA HAMM won the US Female Player of the Year award five years in a row.

In 2011–2012, **LIONEL MESSI** scored 73 goals for FC Barcelona, the most ever in a European season.

PELE helped Brazil win the World Cup three times. The International Olympic Committee named him athlete of the century.

Teams from England and Scotland faced off for the first official soccer match in 1872. The game was a lot different almost 150 years ago. The goals didn't even have nets. They were just two poles with a string running between them at the top. Soccer teams began to use nets in 1891.

Soon soccer spread from Britain to the rest of the world. In 1904, soccer officials started FIFA. The group sets rules for soccer matches between different nations. It also promotes the sport and sets up games. Since FIFA's beginnings, soccer has become the most popular sport in the world. People in most countries call it football. It's not as popular in the United States as it is in some other places. But the sport is growing almost everywhere.

Some soccer matches in the early 1900s drew huge crowds. The crowd at this 1908 match was reported to have more than 120,000 fans!

The World Cup is one tournament where the best players show off their skills. The first World Cup was played in Uruguay in 1930.

You're bound to have your own opinions about the greatest players of all time. You might even disagree with the order of the players in this book. Soccer's long history means that many great players aren't included. But that's OK. Having strong opinions about your favorite players means you're a true soccer fan!

ALFREDO DI STEFANO

Alfredo Di Stefano was born in Argentina, but he became a soccer legend in Spain. Real Madrid is one of the world's most famous soccer clubs. They owe much of their success to Di Stefano. He joined the club in 1953 and proved he could do it all on the soccer field. He scored amazing goals and made exact passes. He played tough defense and never seemed to get tired during games.

Di Stefano's play helped his team win like no other team before them. Real Madrid played in the European Cup, one of Europe's top soccer tournaments. Di Stefano led the team to five European Cup titles in a row between 1956 and 1960. He won the Ballon d'Or award twice, an honor given to the best male soccer player in the world each year. In 1989, Di Stefano won the only Super Ballon d'Or ever awarded. It was in honor of his incredible career.

ALFREDO DI STEFANO STATS

▶ He led Real Madrid's league in scoring four years in a row.

▶ He led Real Madrid to eight league titles between 1954 and 1964.

▶ He led Real Madrid to the Copa del Rey competition in 1962.

▶ He scored 377 goals in 521 total European club games.

▶ He won two Ballon d'Or awards.

FRANZ BECKENBAUER

Good players make the most of their positions on the field. Some great players invent new positions. Defenders used to stay on their own end of the field. That changed when Franz Beckenbauer joined Germany's Bayern Munich club in 1958. He swept forward from his defensive position to attack the other team's goal. He became

known as a sweeper, and players around the world copied his exciting style.

The West Germany national team named Beckenbauer team captain in 1971. In 1974, he led them to the World Cup title match. They beat the Netherlands, 2–1. Beckenbauer became the manager of West Germany 10 years later. Under his leadership, the team won the World Cup again in 1990. Beckenbauer became just the second person ever to win the World Cup as a player and a manager.

FRANZ BECKENBAUER STATS

▶ He led Bayern Munich to three European Cup titles in a row.

▶ He led Bayern Munich to three German league championships.

▶ He was named German player of the year four times.

▶ He scored 14 goals in 103 matches for West Germany, an amazing number for a defender.

▶ He won two Ballon d'Or awards.

MIA HAMM

It took Mia Hamm a while to prove that she belonged at the top level of women's soccer. She joined the US Women's National Team at the age of 15. That made her the youngest person ever to play for the team. But after 16 matches against other national teams, she still hadn't scored. Then she scored in her 17th match. She went on to be one of the greatest scorers in US soccer history.

Hamm was always on the attack. She was fast, smart, and ready to shoot. Hamm's scoring skills helped the US win the first Women's World Cup in 1991. She led the team to another Women's World Cup title in 1999. She also helped the US win soccer gold medals in the Olympic Games in 1996 and 2004.

MIA HAMM STATS

▶ She led the University of North Carolina to four college championships.

▶ She won the US Female Player of the Year award five years in a row.

▶ She won the Women's World Player of the Year award twice.

▶ She scored at least one goal in 15 countries against 31 different national teams.

▶ She retired from the US Women's National Team in 2004 with 158 goals. That was the most goals in US soccer history at the time.

#7

ZINEDINE ZIDANE

To opponents, Zinedine Zidane's fierce stare was almost as scary as his soccer talent. The French midfielder could control the ball like no one else in the sport. His passing and shooting were excellent. Those skills helped Zidane lead France to a World Cup title in 1998.

His fiery style on the field helped make him one of the great players in soccer history. It also got him into trouble at times. He slammed his head into an Italian player, knocking him to the ground during the 2006 World Cup. Zidane was kicked out of the game. It was the last soccer match he played in his career.

But he wasn't done with soccer yet. In 2016, he became the manager of Real Madrid, a team he had been with for six seasons during his career as a player. He led them to three straight European Champions League titles as manager. Zidane proved that he was a great leader on and off the field.

ZINEDINE ZIDANE STATS

► He won the men's World Player of the Year award three times.

► In 2004, fans voted Zidane the best European soccer player of the past 50 years.

► He scored 31 goals in 108 matches for France's national team.

► He scored two goals to help France win the final match of the 1998 World Cup.

► He won the Ballon d'Or award in 1998.

JOHAN CRUYFF

The greatest players can change soccer forever, and Johan Cruyff of the Netherlands did just that. Most teams used a defensive style of play in the 1970s. Every player stayed in position and tried to keep the other team away from their goal. Cruyff and his Ajax club teammates used a new style called total football. It allowed players to move freely around the field.

With total football, Cruyff could attack from his usual position at forward. Then he could drop back and play as a defender.

Total football worked for Cruyff because he was great no matter where he played. He led Ajax to three European Cups in a row. Then he left Ajax and joined FC Barcelona in Spain. He helped his new team win La Liga, the Spanish football league, in his first season. In 1974, Cruyff and the Netherlands national team made it to the World Cup final. They lost to Franz Beckenbauer and West Germany by one goal.

JOHAN CRUYFF STATS

▶ In 1999, he won the European Player of the Century award.

▶ He scored 33 goals in 48 matches for the Netherlands national team.

▶ He scored 290 goals in 514 matches with Ajax and other club teams.

▶ He won the Golden Ball award at the 1974 World Cup finals.

▶ He won the Ballon d'Or award three times.

#5

CRISTIANO RONALDO

Scoring goals is what soccer is all about. Cristiano Ronaldo might be the greatest goal scorer ever. His career as a soccer megastar began when he was 16. England's Manchester United paid more than $14 million to sign him to the team. The investment paid off. Ronaldo was a scoring machine right away. He helped Manchester United win the Premier League title three years in a row between 2006 and 2009.

After the 2008 season, Real Madrid paid millions of dollars to get Ronaldo. He helped them win two La Liga titles. Then he joined Italy's Juventus in 2018.

Ronaldo's playing style is flashy and exciting. With his speed and ball control, he can take over a game. His passes usually find their targets. He plays tough defense, and he's one of the best shooters in the world. He can score with or without help from his teammates, making him unstoppable.

CRISTIANO RONALDO STATS

▶ He scored 450 goals with Real Madrid, the most in team history.

▶ His 120 goals in the Champions League are the most ever.

▶ In 2018, he became the first player to win the Champions League title five times.

▶ His 85 goals for Portugal's national team are the most ever for a European playing for his country.

▶ He has won the Ballon d'Or award five times.

LIONEL MESSI

Lionel Messi is smaller than most pro soccer players. But he plays like a giant on the field. His speed and balance are amazing. He spins and twists and races past defenders. He moves with grace and quickness that other players can't match. He joined FC Barcelona in 2004–2005. At the age of 17, he was the youngest player in La Liga.

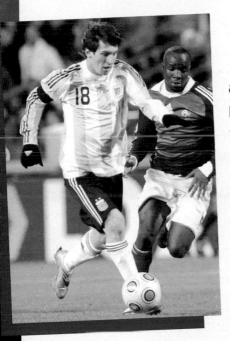

Messi has enjoyed incredible success at soccer's top levels. He helped FC Barcelona win eight La Liga titles. Together, they won the Champions League title four times. At the 2008 Olympic Games, he led Argentina's national team to the gold medal. Messi and Argentina reached the final match of the 2014 World Cup. They lost to Germany 1–0. But Messi's great play in the final earned him the Golden Ball award.

LIONEL MESSI STATS

▶ He is the only player to score against 37 or more top soccer clubs.

▶ He has scored almost 600 goals with FC Barcelona, the most in team history.

▶ His 65 goals for Argentina are the most ever for the national team.

▶ In 2011–2012, he scored 73 goals for FC Barcelona, the most ever in a European season.

▶ He has won the Ballon d'Or award five times.

MARTA

In Brazil in the 1990s, soccer was a sport mostly for boys. But Marta wanted to play. She made balls out of whatever she could find and practiced in the street. She began playing for organized teams at the age of 14. It was the beginning of the greatest women's soccer career ever.

Marta moved to Sweden in 2004 to play for the Umea soccer club. She became the best player in the Swedish league. Marta led Umea to four straight league titles. Marta also starred on Brazil's national team. In 2004, she became the youngest woman ever to score a goal in the Olympic Games. She helped Brazil win silver medals in 2004 and 2008. Marta led Brazil to the 2007 Women's World Cup final match. They lost to Germany 2–0. With seven goals in the tournament, Marta won the Golden Boot award as the World Cup's top goal scorer.

MARTA STATS

▶ She scored 111 goals in 103 league games with Umea.

▶ She was the top scorer of the season in the Swedish women's league three times.

▶ She won the Golden Ball award at the 2007 Women's World Cup finals.

▶ She won 5 Women's World Player of the Year awards, more than any other player.

▶ Her 15 goals in the Women's World Cup are the most by any player.

DIEGO MARADONA

It was always obvious that Diego Maradona was going to be great. He grew up playing soccer near Buenos Aires, Argentina. He tried out for a local junior team when he was eight years old. He was so good that coaches couldn't believe he was so young.

Maradona's play was smart and graceful. He combined speed and power like no other player. Maradona played for club teams in Argentina and Europe. He was very successful. But he played his greatest games for Argentina's national team. At the 1982 World Cup, players from opposing teams bumped into him and gave him little room in order to slow him down. Argentina lost. Maradona led them back to the World Cup in 1986. This time, there was no stopping him. He blew past opposing players and showed that he was the best in the world. He helped Argentina win their second World Cup title. Along the way, he became an all-time soccer hero.

DIEGO MARADONA STATS

▶ He scored 259 goals in 491 matches with club teams in Argentina and Europe.

▶ He scored 34 goals in 91 matches with Argentina's national team.

▶ He played in four World Cups for Argentina.

▶ He won the Golden Ball award at the 1986 World Cup finals.

▶ In 2000, FIFA honored him as one of the two best players of the 20th century.

PELE

Unlike Maradona, Pele's soccer career began slowly. As a teenager in Brazil, major soccer clubs in the country didn't want him. He finally joined Santos Football Club in São Paulo, Brazil. He helped the team win and was the league's top scorer. His success with Santos helped him join Brazil's national team at the age of 17. That's when his career took off like a rocket.

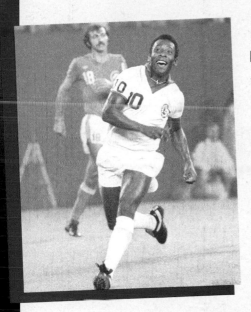

Pele had all the skills of a top player. He could shoot, pass, and control the ball with great skill. But it was his ability to read the flow of the game that set him apart. Pele always seemed to know where the ball was going before anyone else. He scored two goals in the final match of the 1958 World Cup to lead Brazil to victory. He helped his home country win world titles again in 1962 and 1970. His success made him a legend and the greatest soccer player of all time.

PELE STATS

▶ He scored 650 goals in 694 matches with club teams in Brazil and the United States.

▶ He scored 77 goals in 92 matches with Brazil's national team.

▶ He scored 12 goals in 14 World Cup matches.

▶ The International Olympic Committee named him Athlete of the Century in 1999.

▶ In 2000, FIFA honored him as one of the two best players of the 20th century.

YOUR G.O.A.T.

YOU'VE READ ABOUT SOME OF THE GREATEST SOCCER PLAYERS FROM THE PAST AND PRESENT. Now it's time to make your own list! Start by learning more about soccer and the sport's most exciting players. First, turn to page 31 and explore those books and websites. Do you have friends or family members who are soccer fans? See what they think. Maybe a librarian or a teacher can help. Where else can you find out more about soccer greats?

Make your own list of soccer's greatest players. Then ask a friend or family member to make one too. Compare your lists and talk about the differences. You can make other lists as well. Who are the greatest forwards of all time? What are the top 10 best soccer games ever? It's all up to you!

SOCCER FACTS

▶ The first World Cup was held in 1930. Uruguay won that tournament. Brazil has the most World Cup titles with five.

▶ Soccer balls used to be all white. Ball makers added black panels so the ball would be easier to see on TV. Modern balls come in many different colors.

▶ Pele's full name is Edson Arantes do Nascimento. Marta's full name is Marta Vieira da Silva. Brazilian soccer stars often take on one-word nicknames.

▶ In England, a soccer field is called a football pitch.

GLOSSARY

Ballon d'Or: a yearly award by *France Football* magazine to the athlete it believes is the world's best soccer player

captain: a team's leader on the field who speaks to the referee on the team's behalf

club: a soccer team

Copa del Rey: a yearly competition between Spain's top soccer clubs

European Cup: a yearly competition between Europe's top soccer clubs. The European Cup became the Champions League in 1992.

FIFA: the group that governs international soccer

forward: a player who plays near the other team's goal

Golden Ball: an award given to the best player of each World Cup final match

La Liga: the top professional division in Spanish soccer

manager: head coach

midfielder: a player who usually stays in the middle of the field

Premier League: the top soccer league in England

World Cup: an international soccer tournament held every four years. The World Cup is considered the top soccer competition in the world.

FURTHER INFORMATION

FIFA Grassroots
http://grassroots.fifa.com/en/for-kids.html

Greder, Andy. *Behind the Scenes Soccer.* Minneapolis: Lerner Publications, 2020.

Kiddle: FIFA World Cup Facts
https://kids.kiddle.co/FIFA_World_Cup

Savage, Jeff. *Soccer Super Stats.* Minneapolis: Lerner Publications, 2018.

Skinner, J. E. *U.S. Women's National Soccer Team.* Ann Arbor, MI: Cherry Lake, 2019.

Sports Illustrated Kids—Soccer
https://www.sikids.com/soccer

INDEX

PHOTO ACKNOWLEDGMENTS

Image credits: Soccrates Images/Getty Images, p. 4; Bob Thomas/Popperfoto/Getty Images, pp. 6, 7; Bob Thomas/Getty Images, pp. 16, 23, 25, 27; Album/Alamy Stock Photo, p. 8; Keystone-France/Getty Images, p. 9; PA Images/Alamy Stock Photo, p. 9; Popperfoto/Getty Images, pp. 10, 26; Popperfoto/Getty Images, p. 26; Peter Robinson/EMPICS/Getty Images, pp. 11, 17; ullstein bild/Getty Images, p. 11; Allsport/Getty Images, p. 12; Ron Antonelli/NY Daily News Archive/Getty Images, p. 13; Simon Bruty/Allsport/Getty Images, p. 13; Shaun Botterill/Allsport/Getty Images, p. 14; Gonzalo Arroyo Moreno/Getty Images, p. 15; Doug Pensinger/Allsport/Getty Images, p. 15; S&G/PA Images/Getty Images, p. 17; Giuseppe Maffia/NurPhoto/Getty Images, p. 18; Mike Egerton/EMPICS/Getty Images, p. 19; Dave Winter/Getty Images, p. 19; NurPhoto/Getty Images, pp. 20, 21; Jean Paul Thomas/Icon Sport/Getty Images, p. 21; Vladimir Rys/Bongarts/Getty Images, p. 22; Paul Gilham/Getty Images, p. 23; François DUCASSE/Gamma-Rapho/Getty Images, p. 24; Mark Leech/Getty Images, p. 25; Gene Kappock/NY Daily News Archive/Getty Images, p. 27; DenisNata/Shutterstock.com, p. 28.

Cover Images: Focus On Sport/Getty Images; Christian Bertrand/Shutterstock.com; EFKS/Shutterstock.com.